Faith, Election
and the Believer's Assurance
by George Gifford
with chapters by C. Matthew McMahon

Copyright Information

Faith, Election and the Believer's Assurance, by George Gifford, with chapters by C. Matthew McMahon
Edited by Susan Ruth and Therese B. McMahon

Copyright ©2020 by Puritan Publications and A Puritan's Mind

Some language and grammar have been updated from the original manuscript. Any change in wording or punctuation has not changed the intent or meaning of the original author(s), and has been made to aid the modern reader.

Published by Puritan Publications
A Ministry of A Puritan's Mind ®
Crossville, TN
www.puritanpublications.com
www.apuritansmind.com

All rights reserved. No part of this publication may be reproduced, stored in a retrieval system or transmitted in any form by any means, electronic, mechanical, photocopy, recording or otherwise, without the prior permission of the publisher, except as provided by USA copyright law.

Manufactured in the United States of America

eISBN: 978-1-62663-378-0
ISBN: 978-1-62663-379-7

Table of Contents

A Summary of Eternal Election 4

Meet George Gifford 12

Preface 21

To the Godly Reader 23

The First Sermon 25

The Second Sermon 40

The Third Sermon 54

The Fourth Sermon 66

Other Helpful Books on Election Published by Puritan Publications 83

A Summary of Eternal Election
by C. Matthew McMahon, Ph.D. Th.D.

"Having predestinated us unto the adoption of children by Jesus Christ to himself, according to the good pleasure of his will, to the praise of the glory of his grace, wherein he hath made us accepted in the beloved," (Eph. 1:5-6).

Briefly, election is a necessary doctrine that all Christians ought to understand. It is a storehouse of assurance, and gives the believer true rest in Jesus Christ. However, we should also be careful of not falling into the danger of being *overly curious*. It is one thing to understand what it means to be elected in Christ, and another thing entirely to try and *exhaust* such a doctrine, or be all-consumed by it.

God's *people* are elected by grace in Jesus Christ (John 15:16, 17:6; Eph. 1:4, 2:10; 2 Thess. 2:13; Deut. 7:6; Isa. 45:4). This "people" is made up of elected individuals.[1] In other words, individuals are elected into

---

[1] Gen. 21:12, 13; Ex. 9:16, 33:19; Deut. 4:37, 7:7-8, 10:15, 32:8; Joshua 11:20; 1 Sam. 12:22; 1 Kings 12:15, 20:42; 2 Kings 19:25; 2 Chron. 6:6; Job 23:13-14; Psa. 33:12, 65:4, 78:67-68, 70–72, 105:17, 19–22, 135:4; Prov. 16:4; Isa. 44:1-2, 7; Jer. 1:4-5; Mal. 1:2-3; Matt. 11:25-26, 20:16, 23, 22:14, 24:22, 24:40-41; Mark 13:20-22, 14:21; Luke 4:25–27, 8:10; Luke 10:20; 17:34–36, 18:7, 22:22; John 6:37, 39, 44, 45, 15:16, 19, 17:2, 6, 9, 21:23; Acts 1:7, 2:23, 39, 47, 3:18, 4:28, 13:48, 17:26, 22:14; Rom. 1:6, 8:28–30, 33, 9:11–18, 23, 24, 27–29, 11:5, 7-8; 1 Cor. 1:26–29, 2:7; Gal. 1:15; Eph. 1:4, 5, 9–11, 2:10, 3:11; Col. 3:12; 1 Thess. 1:4, 2:12; 2 Thess. 2:13; 2 Tim. 1:9; Titus 1:1-2; James 1:18; 1 Peter 1:2, 20; 2 Peter 1:10; Jude 1:4; Rev. 13:8.

a church-body. This body, known as the bride of Christ or "the church," (those called out) are *made up* of *individuals*. Election in terms of individuals is where God's freedom in his choice of Jacob over Esau is the very inequality of his grace. He is gracious to some and not to others by his mere free choice. This election of individuals is an actual election taking place by God's sovereign decree, to bring together these individuals into one body – the bride of Jesus Christ. God once established, by his eternal and unchangeable plan, those whom he long before determined once for all to receive to salvation, and those whom, on the other hand, he would have to devote to destruction, all for his glory. This is founded on God's mercy and will of purpose. Though unconverted men bock at it, reprobation is righteous and just, and set on his incomprehensible yet perfect judgment. When men are elected, they are called and justified by the Spirit in the preaching of the Word. But those who are reprobated are shut off from the knowledge of his name and from the Spirit's sanctifying influence of true holiness, being as profane as Esau was, and left to themselves.

God is free to actively perform both election and reprobation because he does all things according to his good pleasure. However, man is still *responsible* for their sin because they are cognitive and fallen creatures that have rebelled willingly. Man is in bondage and is unable to save himself, or rescue himself out of this bondage. God must give man the spiritual tools necessary in order to believe, and to "see" that spiritual knowledge is attainable only through God's Christ and in his covenant (John 3:1-10).

Election is not from foreknowledge of merit (from God knowing something done by the worthiness of man beforehand (Romans 3:23, 6:23)) rather is because of God's sovereign *purpose*. Election is set in God's decree before creation and not associated with foreknowledge of any human merit. Human worth, then, is completely removed from this since election was determined *before* the creation of the world in Jesus Christ for all those for whom he came to redeem (Eph. 1). Any virtue, then, that comes from a human individual is based on God's sovereign election, and his Spirit working in them as a result of *his* sovereign purpose. Virtue in any individual is the *Spirit's virtue* working Christ into and through a believer.

Men are elected to become holy, not because they already are holy (or worthy). Election by human merit is unscriptural *heresy*. Merits by fallen human beings are completely ruled out in Scripture (John 1:13, 15:16). God's determination of electing people is based solely on his sovereign will. Paul demonstrates that Israel was chosen, but not all descendants of Israel were *elect*. Paul uses the covenantal argument of Jacob and Esau in Romans 9 to demonstrate that election *is not of works at all*. Salvation is then dependent on God's covenant, and his divine election *alone*. Nor was Jacob elected to earthly blessings. Can one, from Jacob's earthly elevation to first born, infer his adoption into the inheritance of heaven? No. God willed, by an earthly symbol, to declare Jacob's spiritual election.

Election into Christ's kingdom is done *by the Father* giving people *to Christ* as a gift, in the *power of the Spirit*. By his free adoption, the Triune God makes those whom he wills to be his sons; he adopts them as such.

In contrast, rejection and reprobation do not take place according to merit – as if man could earn his reprobation before he was created. Rather, reprobation is also a product of the divine will of God. Reprobation and election rest on God's will alone.

Reprobation has been seen by many false teachers as something as not in accordance with the divine will. Election, some say, is acceptable, but reprobation is not. But how can one divorce this from God's will? If God wills the election of one, then necessarily he did not will the election of another. This does not make God a tyrant, since *men are wicked and justly deserve hell*. God's will is the only proper rule of righteousness, not the emotions of men upon the fate of other men. God is perfectly just towards those who are reprobate, for they are fallen in Adam and deserve justice.

God's decree is also hidden in his justice. God's hidden decree should not be mocked because men misunderstand him or are unable to scrutinize his decree since they are finite. They should accept the general reality of hidden mysteries of God as they are laid out in Scripture though they may not understand everything contained in it as perfectly as they would like. To disbelieve it is to argue that such may not be converted.

Does the doctrine of election take guilt and responsibility away from men? This question is not asked because men want to know the answer, but because they want *to excuse the sinner.* God has made everything for himself, even the wicked for the day of destruction (Prov. 16:4). He shows no partiality to anyone. God predestined the fall into sin, predestined Adam to fall, and predestined the fall to affect all men. God's sovereign *might* controls all things, and his providence *governs* all things. To take away his power over all creation to dispose of them as he wills is to take away God *as God.*

This does not mean that men should not work for good, nor does it make God's scriptural admonitions to them meaningless, for the *means* God employs are useful to his end, as well as the spiritual good of the believer.

Those who are elected by God are effectually called and those who are not bring on themselves destruction. The call of the elect is dependent on the work of grace in their hearts. God appoints men, calls them inwardly, and then justifies them. This is done through Gospel preaching which is the means by which the elect are *inwardly* called by the *outward* preaching of the Gospel. The manner of the call is done by grace alone through the power of the Holy Spirit. The word is preached, and then the Spirit of God illuminates the hearts and minds of those elected. Here, God shows his free goodness in the very act of preaching the Word to fallen sinners. Faith, then is a work of *election*, but election is *not* dependent on faith. Election should be seen and understood solely in the work of Christ Jesus alone. If men are truly in communion with God, they can be assured they have been called by him to be elect and in his Son by their fruitful works. In our prayers, then, we should not act as though we must bargain with God, but rather, we should rest secure on his promises for our salvation. Christ is the Surety in which we rest for salvation, and he truly cares for his people and their good. If we truly believe this, we cannot fall away from Christ. But, we rely on Christ alone, and the Father upholds us through the Spirit of God in his continued work to sanctify. And in those works he has ordained for us that we should walk in them, we are further sanctified.

Many are called by the Gospel but few are chosen by God. The call is then both outward and inward. There is the outward call, that falls on all ears that hear the preached word, and the special call (effectual calling) that changes the heart is accomplished by the Spirit on the heart of an elect individual. The reprobate are administered justice, while the elect are given grace. The preaching of the

Gospel in its effect, then, is twofold – it *hardens* the reprobate sinner further and *saves* the elect.

In this very brief overview, which Scriptural support is abounding in the first summary footnote, Gifford is going to further explain election by first attaching the importance of real faith and fruitful works to the life of the Christian. There is no greater question asked among those doubtful of salvation than *how to gain real assurance*. It is not merely about knowing things, but about how that knowing turns to doing. Gifford will explain the importance of this in the first three sermons. Then, after, he explains those primary principles of faith, how that faith is set in the context of election, and the ultimate entrance that the Christian has into the kingdom of God in heaven. How will they know right now that "such an entrance shall be ministered unto" them? They know it through the truth of the word, as it pertains to the work and merit of Christ, and subsequently, through the visible and sure works of righteousness that the Spirit works in believers throughout their whole life. It is not *by knowledge*, or sheer theological curiosity. The work of Christ applied to the soul of a true believer *will have* the fruits of righteousness by the Spirit exemplified in their life.

One would think that in defining and explaining election, Gifford would take *three* sermons to first deal with that extensive topic, and then meld faith in his final sermon to those who by faith believe in the electing power of the Christ. But, in following the manner the

Apostle Peter outlines in his epistle, Gifford methodically shows the need for holiness, and how the true believer who is fruitful *can and should* then set his heart, soul and mind on the electing power of God in Christ. For God has not "called us" to election, *per say*, but, he "hath called us unto glory and virtue." No virtue, no glory. No virtue, no election. No election, no virtue or glory. All this ties into Gifford's systematic elucidation of these most precious and important biblical topics.

In Christ's eternal and gracious power,
C. Matthew McMahon, Ph.D., Th.D.
From my study, August, 2020

Meet George Gifford

Edited by C. Matthew McMahon, Ph.D., Th.D.

George Gifford (1547-1620) was a most excellent puritan divine educated in Hart-hall, Oxford, where he continued for a number of years. In 1582 he became vicar of Maldon in Essex.[2] The *Oxford Historian* describes him as "a very noted preacher, a man admirably well versed in the various branches of good literature, and a great enemy to popery."[3] Mr. Strype says, "he was a great and diligent preacher, and much esteemed by many people of rank. By his labors he brought the town to much more sobriety and knowledge of true religion."[4] He was a decided puritan, and scrupled conformity in various particulars. He wrote with great zeal against the Brownists, and in defense of the church. But all these things were mere trifles, so long as he did not admire the ceremonies, nor come up to the standard of conformity required by the prelates. Therefore, having preached the doctrine of limited obedience to the civil magistrate, complaints were brought against him, and he was immediately suspended and cast into prison. This was in the year 1584.

About the same time, this learned divine, and twenty-seven other ministers of Essex, presented a supplication to the lords of the council. The ministers

---

[2] Fuller's *Hist. of Cam.* p. 75.
[3] Wilkins on *Preaching*, p. 83.
[4] Palmer's *Noncon. Mem.* vol. ii. p. 38.

who subscribed to this supplication were highly celebrated for learning, piety, and usefulness, many of whom were already suspended for nonconformity. In the supplication they express themselves as follows. "We cheerfully and boldly offer this our humble suit unto your honors, being our only sanctuary upon earth, next to her majesty, to which we can repair in our present necessity. And most of all we are encouraged, when we consider how richly God has adorned your honors with knowledge, wisdom, and zeal for the gospel, and with godly care and tender love to those who profess the same. Most humbly, therefore, we beseech your honors, with your accustomed favor in all godly and just causes, to hear and to judge of our matters. We have received the charge of her majesty's loyal and faithful subjects, to instruct and teach our people in the way of life; and every one of us having this sounded from the God of heaven, *Woe be unto me, if I preach not the gospel*, we have all endeavored to discharge our duties, and to approve ourselves both to God and men. Notwithstanding this, we are in great heaviness, and some of us already put to silence, and the rest living in fear; not that we have been, or can be charged, we hope, with false doctrine, or slanderous life; but because we refuse to subscribe that there is nothing contained in the *Book of Common Prayer* contrary to the word of God.[5] We do protest in the sight of God, who searches all hearts, that we do not refuse from a desire to dissent, or

---

[5] Strype's *Aylmer*, p. 110.

from any sinister affection; soliciting a redress of their thought it does not bear out in the fear of God, and from the necessity of conscience. The apostle teaches, that a person who doubts is "condemned if he eats."[6] If a man then be condemned for doing a lawful action, because he doubts whether it be lawful; how much more should we incur the displeasure of the Lord, and justly deserve his wrath, if we should subscribe, being fully persuaded that there are some things in the book contrary to his word? If our reasons might be so answered by the doctrine of the Bible, and we could be persuaded that we might subscribe lawfully, and in the fear of God, we would willingly consent. In these and other respects we humbly crave your honorable protection, as those who from the heart do entirely love, honor, and obey her excellent majesty and your honors, in the Lord. Giving most hearty thanks to God for all the blessings we have received from him, by your government, constantly praying, night and day, that he will bless and preserve her majesty and your honors to eternal salvation.[7]

> Your honors poor and humble supplicants,
> George Gifford, Samuel Cotesford, Richard Rogers, Richard Illison, Nicholas Colpotts, William Serdge, Lawrance Newman, Edmund Barker, William Dike, Richard Blackwell, Thomas Chaplain, Thomas Howell, Arthur Dent,

---

[6] MS. *Register*, p. 330.
[7] Strype's *Whitgif.* p. 158.

Faith, Election and the Believer's Assurance

Mark Wirsdale, Thomas Redrich, Robert Edmonds, Giles Whiting, Augustine Pigot, Ralph Hawden, Camiulus Rusticus, Jeffery Jesselin, John Jiuckle, Thomas Upcue, Thomas Carew, Roger Carr, John Bishop, John Wilton."[8]

When Mr. Gilford was brought to trial before the high commission, his enemies utterly failed in their evidence, and he was accordingly released. This, however, was not the end of his troubles. He did not enjoy his liberty for very long. Bishop Aylmer appointed spies to watch him, and fresh complaints were soon brought against him on account of his nonconformity. Again he was suspended and cast into prison.[9] On this he made application to the lord treasurer, who endeavored to obtain the favor of the archbishop; but his grace having consulted his brother of London, told the treasurer that he was a ringleader of the nonconformists; that he himself had received complaints against him, and was determined to bring him before the high commission.[10]

Mr. Gifford had many friends, and was greatly beloved by his numerous hearers. The parishioners of Maldon, therefore, presented a petition to the bishop, in behalf of their minister, signed by fifty-two people, two of whom were bailiffs of the town, two justices of the

---

[8] Neal's *Puritans*, vol. 1, p. 379.
[9] Strype's *Whitgift*, p. 159.
[10] Strype's *Aylmer*, pp. 111-112.

peace, four aldermen, fifteen head burgesses, and other respectable people. In this petition, they showed that his former accusations had been proved to be false; that the present charges were only the slanderous accusations of wicked men, who sought to injure his reputation and usefulness; that they themselves and a great part of the town had derived the greatest benefit from his ministry; that his doctrine was always sound and good; that in all his preaching and catechizing he taught obedience to magistrates; that he used no conventicles; and that his life was modest, discreet, and unreprovable. For these reasons they earnestly entreated his grace in restoring him to his ministry.[11] Indeed, the distresses of the people in Essex were at this time so great, that the inhabitants of Maldon and the surrounding country presented a petition to parliament for the removal of present grievances. In this petition, now before me, they complain, in most affecting language, that nearly all their learned and useful ministers were forbidden to preach, or deprived of their livings; and that ignorant and wicked ministers were put in their places.

    These endeavors proved ineffectual. Mr. Gifford did not enjoy his liberty for several years, as appears from a supplication of several of the suspended ministers in Essex, presented to parliament, dated March 8, 1587, when he was still under the episcopal censure. It will be proper to give the substance of it in their own words. "In most humble and reverent duty to this high and

---

[11] *MS. Register*, p. 748.

honorable court of parliament, sundry of the ministers and preachers of God's holy word in the county of Essex, present this our earnest supplication, and lamentable complaint, beseeching you upon our knees for the Lord's sake, and the sake of his people, whose salvation it concerns, to bow down a gracious ear to this our most dutiful suit, and to take such order as to your godly wisdom shall be thought most convenient. Your humble suppliants having, by the goodness of God, conducted themselves at all times, both in their doctrine and life, as becomes their vocation, they submit themselves to any trial and punishment, if it should be found otherwise. Notwithstanding this, they have been a long time, and still are, grievously troubled and molested; of which troubles this is one of the heaviest, that we are hindered from the service of God in our public ministry. To this restraint we have hitherto yielded and kept silence."

He continues, "We hoped, from the equity of our cause, the means that have been used, and the necessities of our people, that our suspension would have been taken off by those whose censure lieth upon us. But they neither restored us to our ministry, nor furnished the people with suitable persons to suitors to them, desiring him we might be restored to our former service and usefulness among them; and, notwithstanding our cause has been recommended to them by some of the chief nobility in the land, even of her majesty in her honorable privy council, we have obtained no relief for ourselves, nor comfort for our distressed people. Therefore, to appear before this high and honorable court of parliament, is the only means left to us; that if there be in us no desert of so heavy a sentence, it may please this high court to take such order for the relief of your most humble suppliants as to your godly wisdom shall be thought convenient."

"We, indeed, acknowledge that diverse causes of our restraint are alleged against us; but our earnest desire is, that this high court would by some means be informed of this weighty matter. The chief of them is our refusing to subscribe to certain articles relating to the present policy of the church, that every word and ceremony appointed to be read and used in the *Book of Common Prayer*, is according to the word of God. We declared that we could not, with a good conscience, subscribe to all that was required of us; and we humbly requested to have our doubts removed, and to be satisfied in the things required; but we have not received one word of answer to this day; and their former rigorous proceedings have not in the least been mitigated."

"We humbly pray this high court to be assured of our dutiful obedience to all lawful authority, unto which, as we and our people have been humbled by the ordinance of God, and for conscience sake, with all our hearts, we promise and protest our submission. We seek unto you to obtain some relief for us. And we commit our lives and whole estate to Almighty God, to your gracious clemency, and to the care of her right excellent majesty, ceasing not, day and night, to pray that the blessings of grace and glory may rest upon you forever."

This supplication was signed by George Gifford, Ralph Hawden, William Tunstall, John Huckle, Giles Whiting, and Roger Carr; but whether it proved of any advantage, is extremely doubtful. Most probably they continued much longer under suspension. He lived to a good old age, and died about the year 1620.

His works (which Puritan Publications is currently working to republish) are:
1. Country Divinity, containing a Discourse of certain points of Religion among the Common sort of Christians, with a plain Confutation thereof, 1581.
2. A Sermon on the Parable of the Sower, 1581.
3. A Dialogue between a Papist and a Protestant, applied to the capacity of the Unlearned, 1583.
4. Against the Priesthood and sacrifice of the Church of Rome, in which you may perceive their Impiety in usurping that Office and Action which ever appertained to Christ only, 1584.
5. A Sermon on 2 Peter 1:11, 1584.
6. A Catechism, giving a most excellent light to those that seek to enter the Path-way to Salvation, 1580.
7. A Sermon on James 2:14-26, 1586.
8. A Discourse of the subtle Practices of Devils by Witches and Sorcerers, 1587.
9. Sermons on the first four Chapters and part of the fifth chapter of Ecclesiastes, 1589.

10. A short Treatise against the Donatists of England, whom we call Brownists, in which, by Answer unto their Writings, their Heresies are noted, 1590.

11. A Plain Declaration that our Brownists be full Donatists, by comparing them together from point to point out of the writings of Augustine, 1591.

12. A Reply to Mr. Job. Greenwood and Hen. Barrow, touching on read Prayer, in which their gross Ignorance is detected, 1591.

13. A Sermon at Paul's Cross, on Psalm 133, 1591.

14. A Dialogue concerning Witches and Witchcrafts; in which is laid open how craftily the Devil deceiveth not only the Witches, but others, 1593.

15. A Treatise of True Fortitude, 1594.

16. A Commentary or Sermons on the whole Book of Revelation, 1596.

17. Two Sermons on 1 Peter 5:8-9, 1598.

18. Four Sermons upon several parts of Scripture, 1598.[12]

19. An Exposition on the Song of Solomon, 1612.

20. Five Sermons on the Song of Solomon, 1620.

21. An English Translation of Dr. Fulke's Prelections on the Holy Revelations.

---

[12] Four Sermons Upon Several Parts of Scripture by George Gifford preacher of the word, at Maudlin in Essex. (London. Thomas Judson, 1598), which was the original title of this current volume.

Preface[13]

To the right honorable and my very good Lady, the Lady Frauncis, Countess of Sussex, R.I. her most humble and faithful servant in Christ, wishes all health and godliness, long to continue with increase of virtue and zeal in religion.

I have for a long time wished (right honorable) that I might in some sort be able, if not to recompence which in deed I shall never, yet at the least, to show some token of a grateful mind for all the ancient kindness and loving favor, which I have found at your hands. This has caused me to miss any occasion by which I might have something to present you with, which might tend to your soul's health. For concerning the things which pertain to the body, as honors, dignities and riches, the high Lord of Hosts has given you so much, that though I gladly do it, yet I cannot directly benefit you in them. Having, therefore of late, a kinsman at home with me, who being, somewhat of a ready hand, has taken from the mouth of our preacher, certain sermons which he has preached, which being again overseen and corrected, I thought it was my duty, to offer

---

[13] *The Principal Effects of Faith and the Doctrine of Election* by George Gifford. Four sermons upon the seven chief virtues or principal effects of faith and the doctrine of election: wherein every man may learn, whether he is God's child or not. Preached at Malden in Essex by Master George Gifford, penned from his mouth, and corrected and given to the Countess of Sussex, for a New Year's gift.

them to your honor, as a taste of those fruits with which the Lord feeds us in the country. Being a great deal more bold to do it, because I know they are such as you have long time shown a love to taste of such things. And I trust these shall also come to you as ripe and timely fruits of pleasant and delightsome taste, although they are set before you in no golden or silver plate, but as it were, in a wooden platter. For the holy apostle Paul says, that this treasure is brought *in earthen vessels*. I implore your honor to accept of my poor good will, and to take this my small gift in good part. Which, nothing doubting of, I pray God to multiply his blessings and graces on you, to his glory, and your everlasting comfort. Amen.

Your honor's in Christ,
RICHARD JOSHUA, senior.

To the Godly Reader

Considering that for a Christian, being sick in soul, and desiring to be made sound, sorrowful in spirit, and craving comfort, unquiet in mind, and seeking to be at rest, wounded in conscience, and would be in safety, tormented in thought, and longing for relief, having offended God, and therefore, is punished, visited with affliction, and gladly would be delivered, there is no other salve but the word of God. And knowing also, that it is the duty of every good Christian in his calling to seek, and thirst after the advancement, and increase of the Kingdom of Christ, and the overthrow and utter confusion of blindness, error, popery, superstition, and to be short, of all the power of Antichrist. I have thought it my duty, rather, (gentle reader), to request this, by various godly men who are my friends, that the preacher of this work to publish this book containing various points of doctrine tending to the comfort of the godly, and the assurance of their salvation. And in it are also diverse confutations of sects and heresies, which to the one reading it with a well-disposed mind, shall be no less profitable, then it is brief. Do not marvel at its shortness. The cause of this is that the repetition in the beginning of every sermon, to avoid tediousness, is omitted. Do not look for (I pray you) finesse of speech, or eloquence in its reading. But way the matter deeply, and apply it to yourself effectually, that you may reap profit out of it, to your soul's health and comfort, that God may grant you this, for his Son Jesus Christ's sake. Amen.

To the Godly Reader

Yours in Christ,
RICHARD JOSHUA, junior.

The First Sermon

"Simon Peter, a servant and an apostle of Jesus Christ, to you which have obtained like precious faith with us by the righteousness of our God and Savior Jesus Christ. Grace and peace be multiplied to you, through the acknowledging of God and of our lord Jesus according as his divine power hath given unto us all things that pertain unto life and godliness, through the acknowledging of him, that hath called us unto glory and virtue. By which most great and precious promises are given unto us, that by them you should be partakers of the divine nature, in that you flee the corruption which is in the world through lust," (2 Peter 1:1-4).

Before we begin to expound on this text, we should note when and to whom this epistle was written. Concerning who Peter is writing to, he states in 2 Peter 3:1 that this epistle is written to the same people he wrote the first epistle to, "This second epistle I write unto you, beloved, in which I stir up your sincere mind, by putting you in remembrance." These were the Jews who were scattered abroad in the dispersion through diverse countries (as mentioned in 1 Peter 1). The Jews were placed particularly under Peter's charge, as the care of the Gentiles was committed to Paul, "But contrariwise, when they saw that the gospel of the uncircumcision was committed unto me, as the gospel of the circumcision was unto Peter..." (Gal. 2:7). This epistle was written by Peter in his old age, toward the end of his life (2 Peter 1:14). As for the occasions which moved him to write, they shall appear in the particular handling of the matters.

Let us now come to the words of the text. The first verse has two parts. In the first part Peter establishes his own dignity – that he is not only a servant of God, but a principal servant, and one who comes to them as the ambassador of God, so they might know the importance of hearing and submitting themselves to the doctrine and message which he brought. For whatever God spoke by the apostles, he so guided their tongue and pen by his Spirit that nothing which they spoke or wrote was their own, but altogether his. In the second part he establishes the relationship which those to whom he wrote had with himself. "To those who have obtained the like precious faith with us," though I am above you in my apostolic position and function, you are equal with me and with the rest of the apostles in the chief and principal position we share in Christ, wherein all happiness exists, even our "precious faith."

Here it may be questioned how Peter can ascribe to them a faith equal to his own, seeing he did so far excel them not only in gifts and graces, but also in knowledge and strength of faith. The answer is easy enough, namely, that this comparison is not made in the measure and quality of faith, for in this some have excelled others far, because God does not give his gifts to all alike. But the similarity lies in its effect, the apprehending of Christ with all his merits, which both a weak and a strong faith enjoy.

Therefore, in this respect, both are equally precious. I share this not to make anyone slothful, as the scriptures urge us to seek to increase our faith. But I say this for the comfort and heartening of the weak, who deeply feel their infirmities and the weakness of their faith. Otherwise, they might doubt whether they were partakers of the same happiness. But on hearing this, they may be well assured even if their faith is no more than *a grain of mustard seed*. Because if it is true faith, it joins them to Christ and makes them partakers in his redemption, having their sins washed away in his blood of righteousness. Their faith covers them with the obedience of Christ and makes them heirs of the kingdom of glory, just as Peter's or any other apostle's faith would do. True faith also provides a sure and stable foundation on which they can stand, even the righteousness of God and of our Savior Jesus Christ.

Indeed, building true faith is so weighty, and the frame so heavy, that it cannot stand on any other foundation but this, that is to say, the righteousness, faithfulness, and truth of God which cannot lie. For if we persuade a man to believe that the thing which we speak has been taught by many different men of great learning and singular godliness, yet because we know that all men are liars, unless we are sure that the things which they speak are from God, we shall still waver, and our faith shall be no faith. True faith rests in the authority of God alone, not the authority of men.

The First Sermon

The second verse contains his salutation, common to him with Paul and the other apostles: *wishing grace and peace* to those to whom they write. And this they do, because the chief scope and principal of their ministry is to bring men into God's favor that they may be reconciled to him. Paul speaks of this same thing in 2 Corinthians 5:18-20, saying, "All things are of God which hath reconciled us to himself by Jesus Christ. And hath given unto us the ministry of reconciliation, for God was in Christ and reconciled the world to himself, not imputing their sins unto them: and hath committed to us the word of reconciliation. Now are we ambassadors for Christ, as though God did beseech you through us, we pray you in Christ's stead, that you be reconciled to God."

This being the chief end of their ministry, they earnestly pray that the people they are sent to minister to know God's grace and peace. They are not only concerned with teaching them this generally, but also directing them in *how* to do the same, not only in their doctrine, but in their lives also. Whoever casts his eyes aside from this goal and end of his ministry, ceases to be the minister of Christ. For example, if he preaches the gospel to seek renown or wealth for himself, instead of seeking this reconciliation between God and men, and to have grace and peace multiplied upon them, he may sometimes preach the truth, but not truly.

Likewise, those parents who teach their children with this mind: "My son shall live an easy and merry life, he shall get promotions and high positions in the church," lay a corrupt and rotten foundation. They have not learned this doctrine of the apostle who warns against ministers greedily seeking personal benefits instead of caring for and feeding the flock of Christ.

But here it may be objected, how can the apostle wish that grace, the free favor of God, be multiplied on them, seeing that God's love and favor does not increase nor diminish, but he loves and favors always alike, being subject to no alteration or change? This may well be answered in that Peter does not speak here of the grace of God toward men, but of their experience of grace, which grows by degrees from lesser to greater. And because it is so precious, the apostle wishes that it may be multiplied on them. He further affirms that the way to grow in grace is to grow in the knowledge and acknowledging of God and of Jesus Christ our lord.

Verse 3 states, "According as his divine power hath given unto us all things that pertain unto life and godliness, through the acknowledging of him that hath called us unto glory and virtue." This verse fits well with the former verse, to show that the abundance of grace and peace is not without responsibility. In other words, you are not to satisfy yourselves with a scant measure of God's gifts and graces, seeing that a storehouse fully furnished with all things pertaining to life and godliness is offered to you.

Secondly, we observe when he says that all things are given to us by his divine power, that there is nothing for us to do in the work of our salvation. It must follow, then, that these which defend free will do not speak with the same spirit as the apostle does here. The apostle does not say here that all those things which we lack, through the weakness of our nature, shall be supplied, but to show that there is nothing in us at all. We are utterly void of all things which pertain to life and godliness in and of ourselves. For that reason, he does not speak of this repairing or helping us in some part, but of a whole and free gift in every part. He says, without exception, that all things pertaining to life and godliness are given to us by the divine power, and so this doctrine directs all the praise and glory of our salvation to God alone.

Thirdly, it may be questioned why the apostle should say that all things are given to us by the divine power or Godhead, when it is manifest that we receive all things from the manhood of Christ. As he says in John 6:46, 54, "I am the bread of life, he that eats my flesh and drinks my blood I will raise him up in the last day: for my flesh is meat indeed, and my blood is drink indeed." By this it is manifest that life is given to the world by the manhood of Christ.

The answer is easy, that Christ in his manhood is a creature, and therefore has nothing of his own, but whatever is in him that makes him the life of the world and the light of men, housing all the treasures of wisdom. This comes from his divine nature, which dwells in his body, as Paul states. Now the reason all these are put into the manhood of Christ is so that we may be partakers of them, for as long as they have residence only in God, we are so far removed from him that we cannot approach or come near him to draw out of him any drop of the same. Therefore, though all things are given to us by this means, God put them into the flesh of Christ, which can come near to us that we may apprehend him. Nevertheless, because the propriety of such remains in the divine nature, their gift is here ascribed to the power of God.

Fourthly, we note in this verse that the apostle briefly addresses the end of religion. All these gifts which pertain to life and godliness – glory and virtue, and all other gifts – are found *in* Christ. That which he expressed first by life and here by glory, that which he first called godliness and here calls virtue, these combine for eternal happiness and life with glory. And the way by which we attain these is the way of godliness and virtue.

Here we should take heed that we do not separate those things which the Lord himself linked together. And this admonition is so much more necessary because there are many carnal professors and abusers of Christianity, which very willingly embrace the promises of the gospel concerning redemption and eternal life purchased in Christ Jesus. They boast that they deserve to share in the benefits of Christianity as well as anyone, and yet they give no attention whatsoever to godliness and virtue, through which we must pass to obtain these blessings. For God has called us to glory and virtue, so that those who know him aright and in truth are made heirs of eternal glory by him. He has also blessed those who are his with virtues and graces of the Spirit of sanctification. So, until such a time as *another Peter* should rise up to write a new and contrary gospel, these men can never assure themselves or persuade others that they shall ever come to the kingdom of God, seeing as they walk quite a contrary path.

Verse 4 states, "Whereby are given unto us exceeding great and precious promises: that by these ye might be partakers of the divine nature, having escaped the corruption that is in the world through lust." Now Peter shows by what means or instruments the divine power bestows those gifts on us, which are those "great and precious promises" given us by God, by which we are called to glory and virtue. They are "great and precious," because the greatness and dignity of what is offered to us in the gospel of Christ is an incomparable treasure, namely, the remission of our sins in the blood of his son, deliverance and freedom from the bondage of Satan and the powers of darkness. We who were once damned creatures and children of his wrath, God chose to grant the high dignity of becoming his sons and daughters (Rev. 1). Christ washed us in his blood and made us kings and priests to God his Father. What a difference this is from the lowest misery, even the gulf of hell, to be lifted to the highest dignity, to be glorified with God in the kingdom of heaven! Because these things are the greatest and most honorable, Peter calls the promises of the gospel "most great and precious."

In doing so, Peter ascribes all the benefits of Christianity to the doctrine of the gospel. When he says that by these we are made partakers of the divine nature, he includes all, because it is by the gospel that we are called home to the Lord. Although his will is revealed in his law, without the grace of the gospel, God is seen only as a severe judge that passes the sentence of our dreadful curse and the vengeance of the eternal fire of his wrath upon us. Though the brightness of his holiness is seen in his law, we are not able to behold it because there is no hope of redemption found in the law. On the other hand, in the gospel God reveals himself in the face of his son, demonstrating his exceeding glory with such fatherly love and pity and such abundance of mercy with which he calls us and draws us to himself. Here we are able to look on him *with open face*. Here his countenance is so welcoming that the soul which catches a mere glimpse of him through the eyes of faith is so inflamed and stirred with desire that it can never be satisfied. For this reason, Paul compares the ministry of the law and the ministry of the gospel in 2 Corinthians 3. He shows how the law is the ministration of death and the letter which kills, compared to the gospel which is the ministration of the spirit which gives life. We should note that this is not the same thing as those who call the true and sound interpreting of the word, "the literal sense," or "the letter which kills," and their own gross and foolish allegories "the spirit." Peter makes it very clear that what he is referring to here is the difference between the law and the gospel. In this is also found what price and dignity the gospel holds. Who can truly determine its worthiness, for by these promises we are made partakers of the divine nature? We were indeed created after the image of God, and so were partakers of his nature. But we lost all this dignity with our first parents, and instead were made partakers of the devilish nature, bearing his image and fulfilling his lusts. Now, by faith in the gospel, this image is restored and built up in us again, and we receive the Spirit of sanctification with the same. If men could understand that all happiness is found in being made partakers of the nature of God, and communicating with him, and that this is possible only by the gospel, men would not despise it so, preferring every little commodity and trifling pleasure before it. Men would not seek to disgrace and slander it. They would not be so soon weary of hearing it, nor think every hour seems like ten when they are listening to it. And finally, unless they were mad men, they would not think themselves best at ease when it is furthest from them. Who willingly throws himself headlong to destruction? Who but those who have tasted so little of its sweetness will refuse to be made partakers of his heavenly nature?

Some heretics say that the very essence and substance of God is transfused into men, causing his substance and theirs to mingle together. But that is not the image Peter is describing here. Peter states that we are made "partakers of the divine nature." If we ask what the nature of a horse is, will a man answer that he is made of the earth, so a horse and a man are both of one nature since man is also made of the earth? In the same way, none is so foolish to think that when we speak of the nature of anything, we are not referring to the substance but the qualities and properties. Therefore, when Peter here refers to the divine nature, nothing else is meant except that there should be such a nature and quality in men, as may carry a resemblance of the divine nature. For example, God is holy, so we must be holy. He is pure, good, just, gracious, bountiful, loving, and merciful, so all these and such like must also be found in us. We shall also come to be partakers of life, of glory, of joy, of happiness and eternity. And so, in a similar manner, we are partakers of his divine nature. Those who have received the precious promises, their qualities are agreeable with the nature of God. Those who partake of the devilish nature compare with those who partake of the divine nature in the same way that light compares with darkness, or heaven with hell, or Christ with Belial. Those who practice such shameful and beastly sins, allowing such to reign in them, partake of the devilish nature. Let such deny that they have any communication with God, much less a profession of faith in him.

What is it then that makes a good man? The promises of the gospel. What brings life and salvation? The gospel. Who has embraced the promises and has the true and lively faith? Those who are holy. Who has God called to life eternal, those he loves as children, bearing his image? These are the pure and undefiled. In the last clause of this verse he shows what he means very plainly: if you flee the corruptions which are in the world through lust, you are made partakers of the divine nature, for the more corruptions and filthy lusts cleave to us, the more they separate us from the Lord. So, the more a man despises them and flees from them, the nearer he approaches God, the fountain of all purities.

We should note that Peter makes all corruption and naughtiness in the world to spring out of "concupiscence," or as it is usually translated, "lust." To be holy, we must first learn what this *concupiscence* or *lust* is, which is here said to be "the seat of sin," and indeed is the root and fountain out of which grows and flows all evil that is committed in the world, whether in thought, word, or deed. In short, this is that which is forbidden in the tenth commandment, when he said, "thou shalt not covet." For this is the root and fountain of all evil against men.

When our Savior sums up the commandments, he states that the first and greatest commandment is to love the Lord *with all the heart, with all the soul, etc.* Now when the whole heart is required, sinful lusts are forbidden. Such lusts do not consist in deeds, words, nor mere thoughts, but embody an inner sickness, bred as they say, "in the bones." This is the depth of our original sin, which we have by inheritance from our first parents and bring with us out of our mother's womb, out of which all evil thoughts and desires arise in us. In the first chapter of James' epistle, he says it is the source that conceives and brings forth all sin. "Let no man, when he is tempted, say 'I am tempted of God,' for God cannot be tempted with evil, neither does he tempt any man, but every one is tempted when he is drawn away by his own lust and enticed. This lust when it hath conceived, bringeth forth sin, and sin when it is finished bringeth forth death."

Faith, Election and the Believer's Assurance

The first thing we note here in this doctrine is this: that all corruption is of ourselves, not coming from any outward cause. It is true that Satan is an instrument, as it were the bellows to stir and kindle in us the lusts of sin. But if it were not for this lust that is already in us, he could not bring his causes to pass. These wicked allurements are the means which drive us and draw us into sin, but the cause is inside of us.

A chief point to be observed is that we should learn to condemn ourselves when we have done wrong, instead of looking for someone else to blame. And we certainly should not cry out in blame to the devil, as though if it had not been for him, I would not have done this thing. When David committed murder and adultery, and was reproved by Nathan the prophet, he well understood that the devil was at work in the matter. Not only that, he could have placed blame on the woman who so indiscreetly washed herself in a place that was visible by others. Yet he lets all these go, and instead wholly and fully condemns himself. He takes total responsibility for this foul and beastly sin and says, "Behold I was born in wickedness, and in sin hath my mother conceived me." He says, in essence, "Lord, I cannot seek in any way to be excused, for all this rebellion against thee is conceived and bred in my own corrupt nature. I brought the root of it from my mother's womb." This is a good lesson for us to learn: for as long as we go about like partial and corrupt judges excusing ourselves, trying to rid ourselves of the responsibility of the sins we have committed, we shall never come to any sincere

The First Sermon

repentance. Further, we should observe that all corruption comes from lust, and if we will but truly repent, we can begin to heal our inner sickness. If a man is changed only in his outward deeds and words, and his inner sickness is not healed, he gains nothing – no more than a man who desires to destroy a tree, but does no more than lop off and shred certain branches and twigs, leaving the stump and root behind. For even if they are seen in the eyes of men to be great converts but nothing in the heart has been altered, it is for nothing. There can be many causes which move men outwardly to appear godly, while the heart within remains fraught with loathsome lusts and full of rotten corruptions, making such a one altogether abominable before God. In short, a man can never rightly judge the level of his repentance without looking to the root of the problem that it may be healed. A multitude of men, being as blind as beetles in this point, imagine that repentance is a very light and easy thing which they can have whenever they wish. When a man of wisdom believes this, however, it is a deep matter whose roots are hard to pull up. Such a one should be even more careful in these matters, lest he deceive himself. Look, therefore, every man to his own thoughts, for by them is the trial made: if the thoughts are changed, and the inward desires altered, so that the profane and worldly becomes holy and heavenly, then he may boldly say, "I have a new heart, and there is a right spirit renewed in me. I have repented. I have not played the hypocrite, but my heart is upright toward God.

The corrupt fountain is stopped, so that the filthy, stinky mud does not boil up and rise to the top as it did before."

It may be questioned whether this is sin or corruption, because Peter said that corruption rests in it. The reference in Psalm 51 proves it to be sin itself, as does Romans 5, where Paul states that even infants have sin, because they are subject to death which is the reward of sin, although it is different from the willful transgression of Adam. Therefore, if we had nothing but this – our innate sin nature – it would be enough to condemn us and utterly cast us away.

Let us never cease working, therefore, until we feel a change in ourselves, even in this secret infection of our hearts, for otherwise we shall never be able to flee the corruptions which are in the world, or as James says in the first chapter of his epistle, to "keep ourselves unspotted from the world," so long as we carry the corrupt world in our own breast. Neither can our religion be pure, for it is also said that if any man among you seems religious but does not refrain his tongue, he deceives his own heart and his religion is vain. "Pure religion and undefiled before God, even the father is this, to visit the fatherless and widows in their distress, and to keep one's self unspotted from the world."

The Second Sermon

2 Peter 1:5-7, "Therefore give even all diligence to join virtue with your faith: and with virtue knowledge: and with knowledge, temperance: and with temperance, patience: and with patience, godliness: and with godliness, brotherly kindness: and with brotherly kindness, love."

Among other chief matters, in the former verses Peter has already declared how we are called to holiness and purity through sanctification. The same was expressed in these words, "that by them you may be made partakers of the divine nature, in that you flee the corruption which is in the world through lust." To this he now adds an exhortation, requiring not only that these Christian Jews do this with diligence, but to give "all diligence," to their sanctification. Peter urges us to give our principal attention to a holy and pure life. For if we cannot attain things of this life, which are small in comparison, unless we put our diligence to it, how much more is required of us to attain heavenly things which exceed in dignity? How far most men are from this doctrine, both in practice and in judgement!

First, notice the amount of labor and pain they expend just to gain the beggarly trash of this world, whether riches or honor. They work early and late, day and night, summer and winter, on sea and on land. They wear out their bodies and nearly starve themselves with hunger. They diligently stretch their brains as much as possible to achieve earthly goods. But when it comes to attaining spirituality and godliness, they pass by them as treasures having no value. They are as slothful and careless in spiritual matters as they are diligent in the other. If a man talks with these worldly men, asking them why they so diligently seek these worldly things, their answer is ready, "lest we shall otherwise come short of them, and go without them." But when asked why they do not as diligently seek the greater and more important heavenly things, they typically answer, "we leave that with God, we do not meddle with that."

In this way they transfer all the concern for godliness elsewhere, as though God did not require it from them. We must take heed to what Peter tells us. He teaches us that we will live miserable lives if we allow this to pass us by. We are warned to give all diligence because it is indeed a hard thing to flee from corrupt lusts. If it were easy, then a lesser degree of diligence might do. But sin's grip on us is tight and is not easily shaken. It is deeply rooted, so that unless we dig down very deep to rid ourselves of it, we are sure to leave the roots behind, which will grow and spring up again as fast as before. Yes, even though our sin seems to be dead, it can suddenly be revived. For this reason, we must work without intermission to pull up these weeds of sin in our life. Otherwise, the ground of our heart will soon be completely overgrown again. Those who despise the means which God appointed for us to keep ourselves pure, using them sparingly, will have their heart overgrown with these stinking weeds of lust sooner than realized. Even if some good seed is found there in the form of good notions or intentions to fear and serve God, if the ground of our hearts are not continually plowed and removed of sin and lusts, the good seed will soon be choked out so that it cannot bring forth fruits of righteousness.

But some may object, saying that this does not agree with Peter's former words, "that the divine power hath given us all things which pertain to life and godliness." Here Peter ascribes all to God, taking all from us. But here he tells us we must be diligent, affirming the role of our own freewill in regard to godliness.

We must answer that God works all in all, and he alone is the power that works in us. And yet he does not work as the carpenter or mason works with the logs and the stone, which have no feeling of what is being done with them, and therefore nothing is required of them. Instead God has given us a will and reason which, of themselves, are corrupt and until such time as God renews them, they do nothing but hinder his work in us. Left to ourselves, our will and reason turn us into rebels and enemies of God. But when God calls us and chooses to renew our hearts through the new birth, he moves us to will, to desire, to sorrow, to rejoice, and such like, so that our diligence is required. His work in us makes us desire diligence for spiritual matters.

God increases all gifts and graces in those who diligently seek him. Let us learn therefore, brethren, to put in practice all those things which are taught here, to give greater diligence to more earnestly seek heavenly things rather than earthly pleasures, to labor more for godliness than for treasures and riches that perish. In so doing, we shall be strengthened to uproot corrupt lusts. And God will give us what we need so that we cannot fail. It follows, therefore, to add virtue to your faith. Peter knows what babes we are, how we are unable to guide our steps in the paths of godliness, which is why God not only moves and persuades us to godliness, but it is as if he takes us by the hand and teaches us how to tread every step. Peter rehearses the things we are to pursue when he says, "join moreover with your faith, virtue, with virtue knowledge, with knowledge, temperance, with temperance, patience, with patience, godliness, with godliness, brotherly kindness, and with brotherly kindness love."

Faith must be in place first, and then all other characteristics of godliness are added to it because without faith we cannot in any way or by any means please God. Faith alone is what justifies us before God. But once true faith is born in a man, it does not remain there dead and fruitless. Virtue is added to a lively faith, that one may attend to all the duties of a godly life. If the faith that is professed is a dead faith, unable to justify one before God, it cannot be considered anything but a shadow or a mere image or picture of faith, having some resemblances of show and color to true faith but not its substance. A skillful painter can cast colors in a painting of fire that at first glance may appear to be real. But even a child can tell it is not the real thing if he holds his hand close to it, because the effects are lacking. There are a very many men, cunning as any painter, who make a show of faith through great boasts and stories about how God is their God, and that they put their whole trust in him in order to be saved as well as the best. But do not let their words and outward appearance deceive you. Rather, apply the true test of faith to see if there is as much virtue in their life as there is heat in a true fire. If so, then know that it is a true faith. For you can no more separate fire from true heat than you can separate virtue from true faith. Godly virtues are the fruits of lively faith. What can be said, then, of all those who manifest so many filthy sins but that they have nothing more than a shadow of virtue. They cannot deceive a wise man, and they surely can never deceive God. So, let everyone examine himself and take heed that he does not deceive himself, thinking he is richly blessed with faith when he is so poor in virtue. For if virtue abounds, faith also abounds. We must try our faith by our virtues.

Next, Peter urges these believers to add knowledge to their virtue. These three are general: faith, virtue, and knowledge, and are inseparable. For faith is not a blind fantasy which man imagines and creates in his own mind, but it begins in the right knowledge of God's will and increases and grows by the same. Knowledge is also the rule by which we measure and guide all virtue. We must not think that something is good just because it seems so to our own reason, but because God in his revealed will has called it good. And until we learn how to live godly through increasing our knowledge of the word of God, we cannot expect virtue to grow in us. This is why the apostle moves these excellent men to increase in godliness by increasing in the knowledge of God.

Note well to whom Peter was writing this epistle. These men are not babes or young converts in the gospel, for he said they had obtained "like precious faith" with him, by which afterward they were established in the truth. We can easily perceive how clarifying this may stop the mouths of many who wish to erroneously affirm that ignorance is akin to godliness and virtue is the true devotion. If this is what they hold, then it follows that their doctrine is false and of the devil, seeing we are charged to add to our virtue knowledge. This is only true if they mean papish devotion, for they could never have kept men in awe, to be zealous of their religion, and to seek honor from men which only God can give unless they kept those who would love God in blindness and ignorance. They chose a wise path to keep the people from knowing the word, which in time disclosed all their falsehood and treachery, so that neither good nor bad has any connection to them.

Then there are those who are not rank papists, and yet they have in themselves still a smack and savor of papish principles. Like fools, they are also enemies of knowledge. Yet they speak and preach, and the people are the worse for it because their words contain no knowledge of God. Peter urges us to learn of God, to take our work seriously, to deal honestly with men.

The Second Sermon

What we are to gain from Peter's instruction is that all men *are commanded to increase in knowledge*, to the end that they may *increase in faith and godliness.* Secondly, let us consider that Peter was writing to poor and rich men, women, and children, to all sorts. In short, to as many as would have faith and virtue, desiring to come to life and glory. Therefore, both the poor plowman as well as the rich clerk is commanded to increase his knowledge of God's word.

Thirdly, to suppose that knowledge, the guider of virtue, should also be the cause of vice is foolishness. If we clear our eyes so that we may look better at the matter, we will see that there is an abundance of spiritual ignorance. Even in those who seem to know a great deal, if the depths of their understanding were sounded to the bottom, they would be found to have only gross ignorance and thick darkness.

So, indeed, the true cause of all wickedness, which abounds this day among us and flows even as a swelling sea, is due to the lack of a true knowledge and understanding of God. This ignorance has taken such root, that all those who know the truth will say with me that our time is like the time of the prophet Isaiah (Isa. 28), who taught the people to the point that he was out of breath with little profit. Yet as the Lord commanded him to continue in his work, he bursts forth, "to whom shall I teach knowledge? Whom shall I make to understand? Those who are weaned from the milk, and drawn from the breasts? For precept must be built upon precept, precept upon precept, line upon line, a little here, and a little there." And in another place he says, "And the vision of all is become unto you as the words of a book that is sealed, which men deliver to one that is learned, saying, Read this, I pray thee: and he saith, I cannot; for it is sealed," (Isa. 29:11).

Further, those who think they have cause to defend themselves when they say, "we are without skill, we have no knowledge, we are poor, honest men with no learning," should instead be ashamed. What they are really saying is, "we have no faith, we have no virtue, we have no godliness." For we are plainly taught here that faith, virtue, and knowledge must increase and grow up together.

Let us all imprint this lesson deeply in our minds, that it may drive us to come out of our ignorance and to seek hard after knowledge. Let us not flatter ourselves as some others do, which having gained some skill, or at least think that they have some ability to teach the word, excuse themselves in this way. "I thank God that I am not ignorant or of the basest judgement. I know somewhat; I am sufficiently acquainted with the matter at hand." Such men are hard to deal with, being wise in their own conceit and not in the Lord. For if they had once tasted even a little of true knowledge, of the sweetness and power of it, they would never have enough. If they had a true hunger for it, they would not be so soon to despise such a wholesome sustenance. Because even when our knowledge is increased, we still only know in part, and we know nothing as we ought to know. For this reason, we are to give all diligence to join to our virtue knowledge, unless when we have begun and proceeded to a point, we may fall back again. This passage plainly tells us the woeful and miserable state of those who being without sound teaching, or having so little of it, come almost to no understanding. They think all is well, and think themselves best, when they are most ignorant of the word. Their merriness is nothing but mad laughter in the face of fearful and horrible destruction.

Next to knowledge we are to add temperance, or self-restraint, as the word which Peter uses here may be translated. But is this not what he means when he tells us to add virtue to faith? It may seem as though he has forgotten what he said earlier, as virtue encompasses all good qualities. We may think he is not well advised, but believes he is talking to babes and children who cannot eat meat unless it is minced and fed in spoonfuls. That is not the case, however. Peter was not simply content with urging these believers to general virtue. He wished to identify certain chief characteristics for which we must be especially diligent. For unless God deals with us in this fashion, we tend to be vain to think we can roam and wander in a wide field and never come near the mark or pursue certain virtues, much less the chief and principal of virtues. Many men speak of virtue and godliness as if their garden is growing full of such fragrant herbs. But on closer inspection, we find only stinking weeds.

In this we find great insight and wisdom, that when we pursue virtue and godliness and call on the Lord to bestow on us spiritual gifts, we should search our life to be certain that while we seek to increase in one virtue we are not allowing another area of our life and spirit to decay. For if we do not look diligently to every area, we may be going backward instead of forward. Negligence in this point of doctrine, or lack of knowledge of it, leads men to a false security. Even though they may show some virtue, they go about it slothfully. And over time, a lack of attention and pursuit of virtue causes men to become slack, as if their godliness were getting rusty. So, if we desire to grow, we must learn continuance.

But why does Peter tell us to add temperance or self-restraint to knowledge? These may seem to have no connection to one another, for temperance has to do with pleasures and delights. But we can plainly see there is sufficient cause for him to join all these virtues together. And we should also note that temperance not only has to do with the delights of the body, but also of the mind. So that in seeking knowledge, which we must do very eagerly, we are to take heed of those extremes which are contrary to a contented mind, either to be so wavering, that every slight wind can push us further from the manifest truth, or else on the other side to be so stubbornly wedded to our own judgment that we defend our beliefs with no consideration for reasonable differences. Both positions are contrary to a contented mind, and both are enemies to gaining true knowledge. Therefore, we are warned here in our diligent search for knowledge, to take heed that when we have learned the truth, we continue steadfast and unmovable in it. We are not to be tossed about, as some unstable minds are, who when they have been taught the truth, tremble and fear when the least doubt is raised against it. We must also not be so blindly attached to our understanding that we refuse to hear wise counsel. James tells us to be swift to hear and slow to speak. Let us be sure our knowledge is well grounded before we settle ourselves to continue in it, lest instead of heaping up gold, we fill our chests with nothing but dross. We also must see that we pursue knowledge that serves to increase godliness and true edifying. For many seek knowledge simply for their vain brain to come up with curious questions without consideration for those questions which would do them most good.

    Next, Peter tells us to add to our temperance patience. This also may seem to be somewhat strange, but if we look at it well, we can perceive the meaning more clearly. Patience is not only requisite in those who receive the profession of the gospel to be able to bear and endure persecutions and afflictions. For unless our hearts are well stayed and seasoned with patience, we may be driven to forsake our knowledge of God during such times. But it is also necessary to be well armed with patience when we encounter those who want to defy the word. For patience is like a dagger to a man's heart who insults and rails against and mocks the plain truth that is so evident before them. They boldly rant and abuse God's word and with their arrogant presumption they would make shipwreck of our patient spirit and so mar and disgrace the gospel we hold dear. Wicked men spew anger and bitterness in an attempt to dishonor God. But we can, in turn, honor him when we patiently remind those of a contrary mind that God offers to bring them out of the snare of the devil to whom they are held captive, if they will but repent.

To conclude this matter, seeing that we suffer for believing the truth, and that we are subject to many reproaches, railings, taunts, and mocks at the hands of absurd and evil men, whoever desires to walk in the way of knowledge must seek to possess patience in his soul.

Next, Peter instructs us to add to our patience godliness. A man may question why we are to add godliness to patience, and then brotherly kindness to godliness, when godliness seems to encompass all these characteristics. It is true that "godliness" usually refers to all goodness, but in this passage, it speaks to something more specific.

Along with being patient, we are also called to be devout or *zealous*. We cannot become so patient that we forget to defend our Lord and his truth. Peter would not have you be so meek as to put up with everything without also being zealous for the Lord. For if God is dishonored, his truth defaced, his servants slandered, and we stand by watching, then that sort of patience has no part in godliness. We must learn to deal in the Lord's matters with not only patience but also with fervent zeal, lest this excellent virtue of patience becomes nothing but a profane ungodliness and an irreligious mildness.

The Second Sermon

Are we not commanded to be gentle? Is it not our duty to maintain love and charity with our neighbors? If they speak against God's word, they shall have to answer for themselves and if we reprove them, they may not take it well.

Therefore, I think it is best not to disquiet them in reproving them. Here is now the exercise of wonderful patience. When men act treacherously towards God and men, this is intolerable. But how do men act in this? For if there are any of them, which being slandered with some foul crime, by which they should receive great injury, or be spitefully railed on, if some of their near friends sit by and hold their tongues, when they know them to be injured by slander, this creates a terrible rift between them. They will say, this is a cold friendship, that they could not have dealt so unlovingly towards their friends when they were slandered, and not stand up for them, even when they heard they were so abused, and yet, they still held their tongue. They should have, instead, imitated God, and his truth in real patience. If they do not, they are not God's friends, and are not of their dear friends, that they can put up with such injury done towards a "friend." There is plenty of this *false patience* in every place, but godliness cannot be suffered to come near it. For if a person breaks peace and is a very unpleasant fellow, he is over rough and over critical to others. There was good neighborhood and friendships before he came. They could be merry together, and be in unity, without any anger. Would it have not been better to use gentleness and patience, then to have this kind of a fight between people? For there is nothing better than love, and where that does not exist, there is nothing good. O! miserable days! The world has an odd view of this love, for they think there is good love now among men. But they cannot really love one another, and they truly hate God. They have a false peace and concord with men, and yet, they are at odds with God. What will they do when God's name is used wrongly, or sinfully? They will, for men's sake, put up with dishonoring *his* name, simply to continue in patience. When they do this, we find that godliness is lacking in them because they do not stand up for God, and, merely for the sake of peace, they keep the peace even when wickedness abounds and love is shunned.

The ungodly world and the wicked nature that is in men take such opportunities to abuse godly zeal under this pretense. They find fault with the preaching of the word because they say it causes strife between men and puts them at odds with each other. But as Peter tells us, we must learn to add godliness to our patience, for otherwise we shall be found to be nothing but irreligious and profane dogs.

The time will not allow us to handle the rest of this text in this sermon. But let us remember what has been said, and give all diligence to pursue these excellent virtues, so that we may approve ourselves to be right Christians, looking for the blessed hope promised in Jesus Christ.

The Third Sermon

2 Peter 1:7-9, "...and with godliness, brotherly kindness, and with brotherly kindness, love. For if these things be with you and abound, they will make you that ye shall not be idle, nor unfruitful, in the knowledge of our Lord Jesus Christ. For he that hath not these things is blind and does not see afar off and has forgotten that he was purged from his old sins."

The Apostle says, *and with godliness, brotherly kindness, etc.* We have heard already that our faith must be joined to virtue or godly deeds, which it cannot be without if it is a true faith. And to our virtue we are commanded to add knowledge. Our knowledge must be accompanied by temperance, and with temperance must come patience. These all join together to characterize *godliness*.

Two branches of these special virtues remain which we are urged to pursue. The first of these is brotherly love or kindness, which must be yoked with godliness. As I mentioned earlier, this godliness Peter speaks to is referenced in the first table of the law, concerning God and true religion, and we are to be sound and zealous in the same. The godliness referred to here concerns the second table and is a godliness that we owe to men. This is very fitting, and necessarily added, for many are only concerned with how to please men, how to not grieve or offend them, while altogether forgetting their duty toward the Lord. In so doing, they wholly shut God out, as though their chief care should be for men.

There are also those who offend on the other hand, those who are always looking to respect the Lord and his truth. While being earnest and fiery in that respect, they overlook their duties to live godly before men as well. We see here that Peter addresses this situation when he tells us that we must so love God that we also love men. He tells us to add brotherly kindness to our godliness. Unless these two are found together, accompanying our zeal for God's word, it is *not* true godliness. It does not matter that we are sound in our judgment and seem to be as devoted as Moses or Elijah in our zeal for God, without a demonstration of godly love to men it does not proceed from God's Spirit. Rather, it proceeds from some corrupt source like vain glory or self-love or such like, and does not deserve to be called godly devotion, no more than true faith can be without virtue. It does not deserve to be called anything but a shadow, or an image of faith if it is without good works. True zeal carries with it a love and care towards men. To be genuinely zealous in spirit is a singular and special gift of God, and they who are without it are brutish and senseless creatures, not knowing God nor how precious his glory is.

This truth must be imprinted on every one of us, that if we love God, we must also love men who bear his image. If we delight in the word of God, one chief doctrine taught in his word is that we are loving and kind toward men. As Paul says in 1 Corinthians 13, the most excellent gifts do not profit without love. Likewise, in this passage we are taught that if we would be godly, but do not have love, it is worth nothing. Let every man therefore stamp this doctrine in his heart, in order that he may be earnest in the cause of the Lord, zealous in religion, preferring God and his truth before all men, whoever they may be. Then he will render to men their due also, and in so doing he may know he is in the right way.

To this brotherly love we are charged to join *love*. It may be questioned here as to what the apostle is doing, for is not brotherly kindness and love all one and the same? Certainly, Peter is not telling us to add two of the same things together, so there must be some difference between the two. In looking at the differences, we might say the first of these expresses what we owe to our Christian brethren, and the latter what we owe to all people, both good and bad. Another consideration is that the former signifies the inward affection of love and the latter, the outward practice of the same.

If we take the former sense, we are charged to join our love for our godly and faithful brethren (whom we ought to favor more dearly) with a love that extends to all: good and bad, friend and foe. Paul teaches this same principle when he tells us to *do good to all men, but especially to those who are of the household of faith*. For this reason, we must acknowledge that we are bound to love even the wicked, as our Savior teaches in Matthew 5, "Bless those who curse you, pray for those who hate and persecute you," and Paul tells us in Romans 12, "If your enemy is hungry, feed him; if he thirsts, give him drink." This goes against man's nature, yet the Lord requires it from us. So, if this is lacking in our daily practice of life, we are only deceiving ourselves as to the integrity of our faith.

If we take the meaning of this charge in the latter sense, which is that the first word signifies the inward affection of love, and the other, the outward practice, then we have here a notable point to be observed. We should not judge our love to be right and sincere, then, when it is halting and lame. For we are charged to love our neighbors, so unless we demonstrate a genuine love for others, we cannot say honestly before God that we love him. Look no further than this, if you bear a grudge or ill will in your minds against another, but say, "I hurt no man, nor I mean no hurt to any," you may try to persuade yourselves that this is an excellent love, in the same way a mere stone meaning no hurt may be said to love.

So do not only look at whether you feel ill will toward another but also determine whether you have any sense of affection in your heart. Going a step further to see whether kindness breaks forth into good and charitable deeds is the real clue. For there may be some loving affection in a man, and yet that affection yields almost no fruit because there is a laziness in his nature that hinders him from putting forth the effort to truly love others. As Paul says in 1 Thessalonians 1, "we labor in love." Love sometimes requires hard work and is *often painful*. So here is the proof of our love, that we do not spare any labor or cost, and that we do not grow weary in love, because love is not found in one who is lazy, loitering at home. But rather it is to be found when one is diligently working to help as many others as he can.

Neither does love prefer and pursue vain pleasure before the benefit of the brethren. By this we know that all those who seem to be godly, and yet will not put themselves out to care for their brethren in need (they will neither travel nor sacrifice for another's sake), they do not love indeed. It is preposterous to show tenderness over a dead body, and to pity the misery of one's passing this life, while having no concern for what is more precious, namely the soul, the renewing and healing of which shall be the happiness of the whole man forever. I say this because we see many that will aid in the relief of some bodily misery, while having no pity on those who wander in blindness and ignorance of the truth of God, whose souls are famished for a lack of spiritual nourishment and full of deadly wounds and sores caused by the chains of sin, held captive by Satan, ready to be swallowed up into the bottomless gulf of hell. The problem with such men is that they have not yet learned to pity their own souls, and therefore, cannot pity the souls of their brethren. For if they truly understood the depths of spiritual misery, they would neither spare night nor day in laboring to have it eased. And yet, to the contrary, they withdraw from men, from godliness, and even discourage them from seeking after salvation. They laugh and sport themselves in their own sins and in the sins of their neighbors, as though there were no misery in them.

Being cruel murderers of souls, any bountiful charities they share lack the authenticity of godly love. So, while we are learning to show kindness and concern for the bodily necessities of men, let us not forget especially, and above all, to pursue with all diligence, as much as possible, the salvation of their souls; otherwise we can never be said to join love and godliness together.

The next four verses share with us both the great and singular blessings that we shall reap if we are characterized by these virtues. Peter also tells us what we can expect if we are found lacking in the same. In doing so, he does not rely on the virtues alone, being so precious and excellent, to move us to godliness. Rather, we are often slothful and dull of spirit, needing to be spurred and pricked with the truth in order to apply it. For this reason, let us be careful to take heed to what he says, "For if these things be in you, and abound, they make you that ye shall neither be barren nor unfruitful in the knowledge of our Lord Jesus Christ." Here Peter begins to discuss the spiritual benefits which will abound in us when we are diligent to be adorned with these graces, "you shall not be idle, nor unfruitful, in the knowledge of our Lord Jesus Christ."

It is a shameful thing to be idle and unfruitful when God has shown himself to us through his Son and called us out of miserable bondage into his service. If the Lord has planted us, if he has dressed us, then, as it is said by our Savior Christ in John 15:8, "Herein is my Father glorified, that you go and bring forth much fruit." For this reason, one can make a sure and infallible argument that if a man is idle, slothful in his profession of faith, cold-hearted, slack in the worship and service of God, and unfruitful in good works, then it is quite apparent that he is *void of faith and those virtues* which accompany *true godliness*. Peter plainly states that "if these things be in you, you shall not be idle nor unfruitful." It necessarily follows, then, that those who are idle, lacking godly zeal, unfruitful, and continuing in their sins have never come to the true knowledge of Christ. They may even boast of their strong faith and make a brave show of their skill and wit, so that men might think there is some deep mystery in them. Further, they may be able to judge and give a right verdict in all matters. But based on this passage, if they are idle and unfruitful in good works, even a simple man can see that they do not as yet know Christ because they lack those former things.

We must note this also, when he says, "if these things abound in you...." In other words, we should not be content with a scant and bare measure of faith, virtue, knowledge, and the rest, but we must labor to have a daily increase. For God moves forward those ripe and grounded men of faith. This is a most notable doctrine, that if men have gone two or three steps, if they have begun only a little to labor about these things, so that they can look back and see some distance behind them, they can know that they are not without faith. By and by they may persuade themselves that they are sufficiently fruitful.

The apostle tells us another thing here from the Lord, which is that we must overflow in these, and abound. These men who think they have enough faith, and therefore seek no further increase of such, have nothing. For if they had ever found the sweetness of these blessings, they *could never be content with so little.* Who is he that, when increased with worldly treasures, cries "I have enough?" Is there less in the heavenly treasures to draw men to them than in the earthly? Or is it because men do not know them? We must learn to take heed of such therefore, that it is sufficient, and even the best of all, for men to be content with some civil decency and not to weary their minds to gain knowledge. There are men who might be rightly called the scholars of Christ and teachers of others, who go contrary to the holy apostle of Christ, who tells us to seek for such great abundance. Such men would be content with, and persuade others to be content with, a mere shadow of those things which, in fact, they should be so fond of. Nevertheless, they are blind, having no shadow or show at all of goodness, and yet believing they have grown far enough.

In the next verse Peter states, "he that does not have these things is blind, and sees not afar off, and has forgotten that he was purged from his old sins." Here Peter demonstrates the hardships which come with the lack of these virtues. He does this because some men will be little moved by the blessings which he spoke of, and will even say, "what do I care if I am idle? What does it matter to me if I am unfruitful? I do not try to be better than other men, so why should I labor to excel those who are wiser than I am?" If it is not important to them that these virtues will make them excellent servants of God, let them consider what the apostle tells them otherwise. Without these virtues, he first affirms that they are *blind* (a miserable physical condition, and much more miserable when it is a spiritual malady as Peter refers to here). God has so clearly revealed himself in the face of his Son and in the knowledge of salvation. And yet, Paul states in 2 Corinthians 4 that the *god of this world has so blinded their minds that the light of the glorious gospel of Christ, the image of God, cannot shine unto them.*

Secondly, he says they cannot see far off. They can see well enough, close enough, but not far off. It may be asked what he means here, since at first, he says they are completely blind and then afterward he attributes some sight to them. It may seem by this that he makes their cause not so evil, whereas before he said it was. But when he states that they cannot see far off, he is saying they have no sight of heavenly things which are removed from us and seen only by faith. He is not saying they cannot see those things which are at hand, because they have sharp enough sight for seeing the things of this world. But he is stating that their condition is no better than that of the poor beast, and yes, even much worse when their misery in the world to come is considered.

Do not let this indictment cause them to become angry, just because they can see *earthly* things piercingly well. But they are as blind as beetles regarding heavenly things. Here we must seek to have eyes given us of God, with which we may be able to see beyond this world. For before such time as the Lord gives us a glimpse of heavenly things, we shall *never* desire to obtain them. And this is the reason these poor blind men never come to know the gospel of Christ.

Thirdly he says they have forgotten that they were purged from their old sins. First, he said they were blind, and now he says they are forgetful, and this forgetfulness is so much more shameful because it is in regard to a chief and principal point of true religion. But where shall we find the man who, when examined, will confess that he has forgotten this point? It seems none do forget it, because the very wicked seem to base everything upon this score, that their sins are purged and this, they believe, gives them the freedom to continue in sin. But if we understand the apostle well, we shall find very many which have forgotten this point.

Now here we must first note that our sins are said to be purged when satisfaction is made for them by redemption in the blood of Christ. And secondly, they are said to be purged by grace of sanctification when by the power of God's Spirit, sin and all sinful affections are suppressed and killed in us. There is a purging in redemption, and there is also a purging through sanctification. They have not forgotten the purging of their sins by redemption, and yet have forgotten that they were redeemed to the end that they should no longer serve sin but purge away the old leaven. Being without those former graces, he says they have forgotten this. Either they never learned it, or they did not learn it well. We can see by this how many are *stark blind* because they have forgotten that Christians are called to live in righteousness and holiness of life.

Let us consider the small number of those who have a desire to seek after the Lord, and yet how few of those come to abound in measure of those forenamed virtues. We should not be deceived about ourselves or about others, and we should deny the honorable name of Christian to those who continue in the filth of their sin, those whom our Savior called "profane dogs."

To conclude this matter, none are allowed to be true receivers of the gospel, but those who join virtue with their faith, and with virtue knowledge, and add temperance, patience, godliness, brotherly kindness, and love, and who seek to abound in them. Those who show no interest in these things, or are content with a bare show of them, even if they seem to be worshippers of God and devout persons, yet, *they are deceived according to this doctrine of the Lord.*

Remember that this is the doctrine of God, and not of man. Remember that we must dwell on it, not for a day or two, now that we have heard it, but all our life long we are to bring it into practice. For it is plain and clear that none can be excused if they do not know it and so attempt to stand upon some common faith, thinking they can hide under the shadow of the multitude. God has warned them, so who can pity those who do not listen. If this had not been told us by God himself, we might think, as men commonly do, that a very little godliness satisfies the Lord and that no great things are required at the hands of Christians. These and other such foolish, vain opinions are *heresy*. God tells us that there is no hope for us unless we walk the path of righteousness. Regarding goodness, a man cannot go too far nor offer too much obedience to the Lord. In summary, let none of all these things blind us, for they do blind some who choose to stand in the light of their own faulty wisdom and deny this doctrine of our Lord.

The Fourth Sermon

2 Peter 1:10-11, "Wherefore the rather, brethren, give diligence to make your calling and election sure: for if ye do these things, ye shall never fall. For so an entrance shall be ministered unto you abundantly into the everlasting kingdom of our Lord and Savior Jesus Christ."

As we have already discussed in the previous verses, Peter lays out what we shall gain if we follow his advice, and also what hurt we will sustain if we do not. If we give all diligence to pursue the former things, the benefits are almost incomparable, as we will come to the assurance that we are called and chosen of God. Assurance is an essential element of salvation, for without it there is no right faith, no frank and willing obedience, and no sound joy.

Without assurance, a man's belief is nothing more than a wavering fantasy. He may do many good things, yet they proceed but from a servile mind. He may be able to laugh and rejoice, but this is a desperate madness which in very deed is to be wondered at. For how can men entertain themselves, and yet speak in their consciences of the reality of hell and its eternal flames of vengeance prepared for sinners when they are not certain they shall escape such everlasting torment?

Suppose a man is taken in a robbery or murder, imprisoned, brought before the judge, and condemned. But his friends are able to secure a temporary reprieve for him while they seek to get a pardon issued on his behalf. In the meantime, someone comes to this murderer and tells him he should be of good cheer. Unless he is mad, he will answer "I am condemned to the gallows. The judge has pronounced the sentence of death on me, and I know how difficult it will be to obtain a pardon. For this reason, I cannot be happy until I know for certain that I shall escape. Once I know that, then I can be as merry as any man alive. But before then, I may seem to laugh, but my heart is full of fear and sorrow."

Is it not this way with us all? We are all guilty, already condemned by the sentence of the highest Judge, and not to some torment of one day or a brief while, but to *the fire that shall never be quenched.* Therefore, when men can be merry and laugh even in those things which cause this destruction, without knowing for sure that they will escape such a dreadful vengeance, is it not a *mad merriness and a desperate laughter?* If they were not so dull of spirit, this fact would grip their heart with fear. It would gnaw at their mirth like a destructive worm. It would rob them of rest and joy. If we were no more than desperate and mad fools, the thought of hell would dampen all our mirth until such time as we could make sure we would escape it. Therefore, what the apostle has to say here is an essential consideration. Walking in the way he has prescribed, we shall come to the assurance that we are the called and chosen of the Lord.

You may question how this principle can agree with other sayings in the holy scriptures which plainly teach that God *chooses* whom he will of his own free grace. *God will have mercy on whomever he will have mercy, and those whose hearts he chooses to harden, he will harden.* For this reason, it is not up to us to will our salvation, but it is God's doing to show mercy on those he chooses to show mercy and pardon.

The doctrine of popery says that God makes his choices based on the fact that he knows ahead of time who will perform good deeds. If this were true, election would depend on the worthiness of men. However, this passage does not contradict that free choice which God makes without respect of anything that is in us, for he could find nothing in us that might in any way move him. Neither does this passage prove in any fashion that election is conditional. Peter does not even discuss the doctrine of election in this passage, or what moved God to make the choices he made. Nor does it touch on the certainties and stability of election.

Rather, his purpose here is to teach us how we shall attain this incomparable treasure, to be assured and resolved in ourselves, not by fantasied opinions, but by sure and substantial proof, that we are chosen of God, and therefore, cannot perish. If we respect the unchangeable counsel of God, then here rests the sure foundation of election, because *God,* who cannot be deceived, nor repent or change, *has made the choice.* And those whom he chose can, therefore, never perish. If we consider the way and means by which we may come to know this favor of God toward us, the Lord by his apostle tells us that this is the way, give all diligence and study to learn of him and be richly decked with his graces or those forenamed virtues. For by these we shall gain assurance. If we have these, and if they abound in us, we shall, as he says, never fall.

Let us learn this first, then, that election itself rests on the unchangeable purpose and counsel of God. Then secondly, that we are not to gain assurance of it in ourselves from some personal revelation. Neither are we to attempt to ascend into heaven to search the counsel of God, to determine whether our names are in the book of life. But we are to gain assurance *from the fruits of the Spirit who dwells in us.* Though we must look within in order to judge whether those things are in us which are given to all those whom God chooses, we will gain assurance because of the seal of God by which he has sealed us, which is the Spirit of sanctification.

As Peter said, if you do these things, you shall never fall. Is that because our doings are so perfect and sure, or that we are so confident in ourselves? No, not at all. It is, however, by these virtues that we know we are sealed with God's Spirit, whose working we feel in us. We also know that as many as *are led by the Spirit of God are the sons of God* (Rom. 8:14). Look how with the increase of knowledge comes the increase of virtues and heavenly desires, which causes that man to be assured that he is the child of God. For as one increases, so also does the other. Contrarily, when a man feels within himself an evil conscience, feels that he is darkened in his understanding, led by the lusts of sin, he shall wonder, "I do not know

The Fourth Sermon

whether I am saved or not." And yet, look how the other may say, "I know I shall be saved, because God has sealed me with his Spirit."

We may see by this how beneficial they are, and merciful to their own souls, those who with all their power day and night give up themselves to seek after the knowledge and obedience of the Lord's will. By not failing nor growing weary, they shall in continuance of time, find such a blessing from the Lord in the increase of faith and virtue that will cause them to say, "we have not wasted our labor." On the other hand, we see how unkind and cruel those are to themselves who through idleness and slothfulness in seeking after God cut the throat of their own faith. They cannot truly trust in a God whom they so often disobey. This passage in Peter is a mighty force that overthrows the vanities of various opinions which many men hold. For those who cry out against this doctrine as a thing which will make men careless and idle in the service of God and stop the course of good works, I urge you to mark how well these wise men have profited in God's school, see how they agree with the holy apostle when he says we are to give all our study and diligence to good works if we are to come to the sure and undoubted knowledge that we are chosen unto life. For we cannot come to the assurance of our faith without a great attention to godliness, abundance of virtue, and plenty of all good works.

Some will say, however, that if you want men to be concerned with godliness you must do away with the doctrine of election, for it destroys in men the study and attention to good works. Some others, though not so brutishly blind, think this doctrine is the test for whether we have done well or not. That is, when a man has done many good deeds, he shall know he has not done them well if he still doubts, he is one of God's chosen.

God does not work so darkly by his Spirit in men, but they may know whether something is of him if they would only dutifully judge themselves. For we must not rest in the outward doing of good things, but in the right doing. Let him who gives himself to do good works be careful to fashion them after the rules of the word.

There is a third group of men who will mightily defend the doctrine that men ought to be sure of salvation. They suggest that we cannot honor God more than when we give full credit to his promises, and because the plain testimony of the scripture compels them, they affirm it constantly, and condemn the contrary as a foul error. They say that if God has chosen a man, that man will come to feel and to know this for certain. And because it is a true doctrine, they say also that they themselves are sure that God has chosen them.

But when they do not take what Peter lays down here as *the means for us to become sure of our salvation*, but go in a contrary path and are accused of filthy crimes, we may confidently say that they are *liars*. For although they brag with their tongues about what they should be, there is a bird in their breast which sings a contrary note and tells them plainly what they are.

There is another kind of man which cannot be persuaded in any fashion that a man can be sure of his salvation. Therefore, with scoffs they ask of them who profess the word, when did God tell them so? If it could not be known, then the apostle has greatly overshot himself in telling us how we shall come to be *sure*. But ask a question of them, whether they do not believe in God, and every one of them will answer, "I put all my trust in him." Reason then a little further and tell them that the scripture which cannot lie says that all who trust in God shall be saved. How then will they join these together, that they trust in God, and yet doubt whether they shall be saved? Can God deceive? Undoubtedly if they knew that they had trusted in him, they should also know they cannot perish.

But let us learn from this the misery of our time, in which men still think this doctrine is strange, by looking at the particular application of this doctrine in which everyone must bring home to himself. Remember this, that those whom God has called home to himself and chosen to be his children, he also gives them true faith and a spiritual sense that they are his elect, and such as perceive no such thing in themselves are in a very miserable condition.

Therefore, every man must ask this question of his own soul, "how does this matter go with me? Am I sure God has chosen me? Do I feel any assurance of eternal life?" The conscience will answer uprightly if we are not negligent to inquire. And if we find that the answer comes back, "I am not sure, for I doubt and stagger," we must inquire within ourselves as to what the reason for this is.

Faith, Election and the Believer's Assurance

God is faithful. He has promised eternal life to all who believe. Our heart may answer, "you do not fear God, you are full of foul sins, evil lusts reign in you. You do not study God's word, and you are unfruitful and barren in good works." If this is the case, then you cannot say "I am led by the Spirit of God, and therefore, I am sure I shall be saved." A wise man will not say, as the manner of fools is, that "I am not sure indeed, neither do I think any man can be. I commit it to God, let him do with me what he will." These speeches may seem to have some wit and godliness in them, but they are indeed devilish and mad, because God has taught us a contrary lesson in this passage.

Now ask yourself this question: "May I come to this assurance? And, if so, what is the way?" The Lord answers by his apostle, "You may come to this assurance in this way," and points him in the direction. Here you must travel and go forward. Do not stay idle, but labor, for these men had gone a great way and yet they are urged to continue still. For if the Lord does not give this assurance, we are to labor so much the more, and to be so much the more persistent in seeking for knowledge, to call ourselves to a greater responsibility, to set a watch over our affections to see with what mind we do things, to allow no sin to willingly dwell in us, nor be slack to any good work which God has appointed us. We should cry to God for faith and for his Spirit to guide us, to use the means diligently which God has appointed, which is hearing, searching, and meditating in the word. And in time God will let us see that he is our God, and that neither life nor death, height or depth, things present or things to come, angels, principalities, nor powers, nor any creature shall separate us from his love in Christ.

Verse 11 states, "For such an entrance shall be ministered unto you abundantly into the everlasting kingdom of our Lord and Savior Jesus Christ." This is a confirmation of the last clause of the former sentence, where he says, "if you do these things, you shall never fall." Why? Because you shall have a great entrance into the eternal kingdom of Christ. Peter stated earlier that you are to be diligent *to make your calling and election sure*. But can you be assured of your salvation? Yes, *most certainly*. He that proceeds and grows in his faith so far that he knows he shall never fall away from God to destruction is also sure that he is chosen. For he does not speak of falling into *every* particular sin, which happens to the most godly from time to time. But Peter says, "I tell you that if you do these things, you shall never fall," not because we are capable of keeping ourselves from sin, but because we know that our own good works are the fruits of God's Spirit in us, which is the seal he has set upon all those he has chosen to life eternal. And since God is unchangeable, it follows that such a one shall not fall, for Christ reigns in them, as he does in all the faithful by his Spirit, and they have a rich entrance into the kingdom of Christ which is everlasting. So, his chosen *cannot fall* unless the power of Christ fails, and his kingdom comes to an end; and when will this ever happen? It cannot.

Note that the force of reason rests in the difference between the kingdom of Christ and the kingdoms of this world which, though they may be mighty and full of policies and wisdom, in time they shall all come to an end. Therefore, a man cannot rightly say to the subjects of worldly kingdoms that you have a mighty prince who is bountiful and gracious, your peace, therefore, and happy estate, shall endure forever. No, for the mighty may be overcome, if not by men, at least by death, and so they may be in peace and a good estate today, but tomorrow they can all be in an uproar. Today they may be ruled by a loving and gracious prince, and tomorrow a fierce tyrant. This is the state of uncertainty of the kingdoms of this world. But the kingdom of Christ, whose power is above all and can never come to an end, is eternal, as Peter here states. Because God's state is unchangeable, so is theirs in whom his Spirit dwells, so they can be sure they can never fall.

The apostle makes this matter so clear that we can only marvel how it is that this doctrine of the Lord should find so few friends and so many extreme enemies. But indeed, men who do not have God's Spirit dwelling in them, confess the truth that they do not feel any such assurance, and therefore, cannot stand to hear that all true godly men, faithful Christians, have this knowledge in themselves.

Let us listen to the apostle, who tells us how we shall come to have Christ as our king, and to reign over us, namely if we yield ourselves to the governance of his spirit, which works all goodness in our hearts, subduing and vanquishing all the rebels in and around us. Such wicked men follow their own fleshly minds, and give into the raging lusts of the flesh, despising the knowledge of God's will, and therefore do not regard his word. They may call Christ their King and their Lord, but God says here by his apostle that the entrance into his kingdom is *by following after virtue, knowledge and godliness.* They show that they are not his subjects, being altogether void of his Spirit, but rather slaves of sin and Satan, whose kingdom they uphold with tooth and nail. As those who are of a completely different company who fight against the truth rather than profess it, they devise all the means and methods they can to maintain sin, inventing all the slanders they can to discredit the godly. If God opened their eyes to see even a glimpse of what he is teaching in this passage, they would be ashamed of what they now boast and brag of. They would also confess that, like blind buzzards and mad beasts, they have fought against God and not men. Finally, it would make them change their ways and seek diligently to have the witness within themselves that they are the servants of God.

We must also mark well one other thing which is mentioned here, which is that he says *an entrance shall be abundantly ministered to you* when you have consistently labored for your faith to be soaked and seasoned with godliness and plentifully adorned with all graces and gifts of the spirit. If you proceed so far, and gain so much, that your entrance into the kingdom of Christ shall be very great, it follows that you may be assured of your standing in Christ. You can know that you will reign with him and he will be your king because once Christ's Spirit begins to reign in a man to drive out the power of Satan, he will not afterward cast him to destruction.

But it is not enough to *have* an entrance; we should desire *a rich entrance* into his kingdom. This description is not added in vain, for we are taught to take heed that we do not become content with some little taste and a small entrance. This difference should be made, that though some may have good desires and motions, though they may taste the good word of God and are, in some sense, enlightened, if they are afterward overcome with sinful lusts and vain delights of the flesh, it may be surely said that Christ never reigned in them. On the other hand, those who have the deep roots of sin dug out and in its place planted the good seed of God's word in their hearts, as they live day to day they will go from grace to grace, and from strength to strength, until Christ establishes his throne in them, overthrowing the power of darkness and robbing the devil of the interest he formerly had. This doctrine will do us much good if we believe it.

Considering the nature and disposition of men of this day, they are afraid of going too far in virtue and knowledge, they do not value being admonished or taught diligently, and they take displeasure when they are scorned. They have not learned the first point of a Christian scholar, and are so far from having this abundant entering into the kingdom of Christ.

The Fourth Sermon

Learn this therefore, dearly beloved, and learn it well. Lay sure hold on it and do not let it slip from you, for God teaches us in this passage that the only way to life and happiness is to let go of the vain dreams and foolish opinions of people steeped in their ignorance. They are so blinded by the malice of Satan that whichever way they go, they still hope for eternal glory, as though the way to heaven were so broad that a man could not miss it, and the entrance so easy that he may enter whenever he wishes. This is the *heresy* of our time, that a man will spend his time in ignorance, not caring for, nor seeking after the true knowledge of God. Rather, he allows himself to be defiled with foul and beastly sins, that indeed there is nothing in him but pride, self-love, vain glory, envy, gluttony, the lusts of adultery, and such like, to the degree that the scripture compares him to a swine or a dog. Yet if he has God in his mind, and can say, "Lord have mercy upon me," they think this is all that is required. They will not attempt to pursue or acquire more, not being acquainted with what God tells his people in this passage by his apostle. How far men must proceed in their faith before they can warrant themselves to be fully secure in their salvation. For you may as well join heaven and hell together, fire and water will as soon agree, light and darkness will sooner be one, as join the common faith to what we are taught in this passage.

But I will return to apply this doctrine to the godly for whom it is written. I will share how they can be dead sure of their salvation. Many godly men, which after long travail and much care to please God, are still so entrenched in their stubborn nature and so deeply infected and poisoned with sin, that they are compelled to doubt and to think their labor is lost. Let not this man be dismayed, but let him go forward, remembering what is promised here. The more he desires to grow his faith, the more let him strive. He will soon plainly perceive that God regards his efforts, considers his sighs and groans, and will perform all his desires. Let him remember that these men to whom Peter wrote had obtained *the precious faith*. They knew they were established in the present truth, and yet they were not so far along in their journey that they could not be moved to make their election sure and to seek a further entrance into the kingdom of Christ. So, they were continuing what was begun.

We ought to be moved all the more, because the world is full of fearful examples which, if they were to be well considered, would cause a man's hair to stand upright. There are many who are lacking this doctrine, or at least lack the practicing of it, yet seem not only to have had some good liking of the truth but also a great zeal. These, like good scholars, proceed to the highest form. It is so dangerous to relent or slack in our pursuit of godliness before we have gained this full assurance and make this rich entrance into the kingdom of Christ.

We must seek to be led by the Spirit of God and know for certain that we are Christians, not by any vain conceit of our own foolish brain, nor by senseless security, but by the working and fruits of his Spirit in us. If this were well weighed, men would not be content with so little, or nothing, in this regard. They would not make such a light account of teaching. They would leave their slanderous and reproachful railings. They would not like filthy swine wallow in the mire of their sins. They would not prattle so much of this, that all are sinners, and therefore, think all are alike, throwing together all those who would be godly and faithful with those who would be ungodly infidels, children of the devil, and heirs of hell. Indeed, though all are sinners, there is a vast difference between the two. For some continue in their sins, seducing and deceiving themselves with some vain hope of God's mercy, and others repent after the manner prescribed in it. They cleanse themselves more and more from all filthiness of the flesh, and grow in all virtues and graces, until they are decked in their souls with heavenly ornaments and have yielded up themselves to have Christ reign in them.

As for common repentance, which is to cry only with words for mercy and in some light measure to be grieved or to fear the judgments of God, and yet within the soul nothing changes and the spirit is not renewed, deceives all who trust in it. A sinner can repent and be forgiven, but as Peter describes here, this is as different as an apple is to an oyster. If we look closely at them both, we find them to agree in very few things.

So, let us go forward and not so much as look back, until such time as we have by our own experience proved that what Peter is saying here is *true*. It is not enough to *believe* that this is true (although that is something) unless we try to believe it ourselves. He is a blind fool who sees this as the only way to happiness and yet, due to slothfulness, will not walk in it, as though the kingdom of heaven is not worth the effort.

Further, Peter requires that those who would attempt to bring other men to assurance must have first walked this way themselves. For how can they bring other men to that which they themselves do not have. It also appears that God has rendered judgment against those who attempt to guide others but cannot show them the true path of which this passage speaks, which is the only way to heaven. If God should thunder on them from heaven or send fire on their houses, especially when they are so blind, they may still think themselves to be in a better state than those whom God rules by his word. But *woe to those blind guides and shepherds* who mislead others; and wretched are those people who are as sheep without a shepherd. For how shall they hear of these things? We can pity their misery and pray the Lord to send help for so lamentable and desperate a case, but indeed, most men know nothing. For had they known what God requires in that man whom he will save, though they were not partakers of it themselves, yet they could consent and agree to the doctrine and confess that there is no way to attain eternal life but by sound teaching as may bring people to the things here required.

Oh Lord grant, that this doctrine which you have taught us in your holy word may enter into us and dwell in us forever, that we may be sure of your favor and of eternal

The Fourth Sermon

life through Jesus Christ your dear Son, our Lord and only Savior. Amen.

Other Helpful Books on Election Published by Puritan Publications

The Two Wills of God Made Easy
by C. Matthew McMahon

What is God's will for my life? Does God love everyone? Is God's will ever frustrated? Does God change His mind? This newly abridged version gives the Christian the proper hermeneutical tools to define "God's will" and how his will functions in and through redemptive history. It solves critical questions surrounding God's nature, demonstrating that proper biblical interpretation is the key to understanding the will of God in an easy to understand format.

The Order of the Causes of Salvation and Damnation
by William Perkins (1558-1602)

One of the best systematic treatments of election and reprobation is now available in a more modern version, which includes a PDF and JPEG of Perkins' Chart, both in the book and as a stand-alone file. Perkins' Chart alone is worth your study time.

A Poster on the Synopsis of Theology or Divinity
by Francis Roberts (1609–1675)

This is one of the best learning charts of the Puritan era by Francis Roberts on theology. He created this chart to aid his congregation to understand theology, including the topics of God, the Bible, Redemption, the person of Christ, election, effectual calling, and more. A 40" x 60" chart and masterpiece of theological precision.

Other Works by Puritan Publications

Armilla Catechetica, or a Chain of Theological Principles
by John Arrowsmith (1602-1659)

One of the best systematic treatments of important issues by a Master Theologian and one of the most respected Westminster Divines. This is now in an electronic format that makes studying this work very easy, and it is in modern English.

God's Glory in Man's Happiness
by Francis Taylor (1589-1656)

Election and Predestination are important topics surrounding the manner in which God saves his people. Francis Taylor, an active member of the Westminster Assembly, takes great care in explaining how God saves through Jesus Christ. This is a hearty Reformed treatment of the bible's teaching on God's election of his people.

The Principal Causes of Man's Salvation
by John Brinsley (1600-1665)

In one of the most concise and helpful treatments of election and reprobation by any puritan in print, this work is a gem. Don't miss out on any of Brinsley's works, especially this wonderful treatment of Christ's work to save his people from their sins.

Augustine's Calvinism: The Doctrines of Grace in Augustine's Writings
by C. Matthew McMahon

Did Augustine believe and teach the doctrines of grace? Or were these doctrines formulated later? This work is a survey of Augustine's writings with the conclusion that Augustine was no doubt, a Calvinist.

www.ingramcontent.com/pod-product-compliance
Lightning Source LLC
Chambersburg PA
CBHW070208100426
42743CB00013B/3094